Eating With *Efficiency*

A Meal Planner Shopping List

@ Journals & Notebooks

Copyright 2016

Date : _________________________ mon tue wed thu fri sat sun

	Breakfast	Lunch	Dinner
Monday			
Tuesday			
Wednesday			
Thursaday			
Friday			
Saturday			
Sunday			

Shopping List

Meat :   Dairy :   Others:

Produce:

Date : _________________ mon tue wed thu fri sat sun

	Breakfast	Lunch	Dinner
Monday			
Tuesday			
Wednesday			
Thursaday			
Friday			
Saturday			
Sunday			

Shopping
List

Meat :   Dairy :   Others:

Produce:

Date : _______________________ mon tue wed thu fri sat sun

	Breakfast	Lunch	Dinner
Monday			
Tuesday			
Wednesday			
Thursaday			
Friday			
Saturday			
Sunday			

Shopping List

Meat :

Dairy :

Others:

Produce:

Date : _________________ mon tue wed thu fri sat sun

	Breakfast	Lunch	Dinner
Monday			
Tuesday			
Wednesday			
Thursaday			
Friday			
Saturday			
Sunday			

Shopping List

Meat :   Dairy :   Others:

Produce:

Date : _________________ mon tue wed thu fri sat sun

	Breakfast	Lunch	Dinner
Monday			
Tuesday			
Wednesday			
Thursaday			
Friday			
Saturday			
Sunday			

Shopping List

Meat :   Dairy :   Others:

Produce:

Date : _________________________ mon tue wed thu fri sat sun

	Breakfast	Lunch	Dinner
Monday			
Tuesday			
Wednesday			
Thursaday			
Friday			
Saturday			
Sunday			

Shopping List

Meat :   Dairy :   Others:

Produce:

Date : _________________ mon tue wed thu fri sat sun

	Breakfast	Lunch	Dinner
Monday			
Tuesday			
Wednesday			
Thursaday			
Friday			
Saturday			
Sunday			

Shopping List

Meat :   Dairy :   Others:

Produce:

Date : _________________ mon tue wed thu fri sat sun

	Breakfast	Lunch	Dinner
Monday			
Tuesday			
Wednesday			
Thursaday			
Friday			
Saturday			
Sunday			

Shopping List

Meat :   Dairy :   Others:

Produce:

Date : _________________ *mon tue wed thu fri sat sun*

	Breakfast	Lunch	Dinner
Monday			
Tuesday			
Wednesday			
Thursaday			
Friday			
Saturday			
Sunday			

Shopping List

Meat :   Dairy :   Others:

Produce:

Date : _________________ mon tue wed thu fri sat sun

	Breakfast	Lunch	Dinner
Monday			
Tuesday			
Wednesday			
Thursaday			
Friday			
Saturday			
Sunday			

Meat :   Dairy :   Others:

Shopping
List

Produce:

Date : _________________ mon tue wed thu fri sat sun

	Breakfast	Lunch	Dinner
Monday			
Tuesday			
Wednesday			
Thursaday			
Friday			
Saturday			
Sunday			

Shopping List

Meat :

Dairy :

Others:

Produce:

Date : _________________ mon tue wed thu fri sat sun

	Breakfast	Lunch	Dinner
Monday			
Tuesday			
Wednesday			
Thursaday			
Friday			
Saturday			
Sunday			

Shopping List

Meat :   Dairy :   Others:

Produce:

Date : _________________ mon tue wed thu fri sat sun

	Breakfast	Lunch	Dinner
Monday			
Tuesday			
Wednesday			
Thursaday			
Friday			
Saturday			
Sunday			

Shopping
List

Meat :   Dairy :   Others:

Produce:

Date : _______________________ mon tue wed thu fri sat sun

	Breakfast	Lunch	Dinner
Monday			
Tuesday			
Wednesday			
Thursaday			
Friday			
Saturday			
Sunday			

Shopping List

Meat :   Dairy :   Others:

Produce:

Date : _________________ mon tue wed thu fri sat sun

	Breakfast	Lunch	Dinner
Monday			
Tuesday			
Wednesday			
Thursaday			
Friday			
Saturday			
Sunday			

Shopping
List

Meat :   Dairy :   Others:

Produce:

Date : _________________ mon tue wed thu fri sat sun

	Breakfast	Lunch	Dinner
Monday			
Tuesday			
Wednesday			
Thursaday			
Friday			
Saturday			
Sunday			

Shopping List

Meat :   Dairy :   Others:

Produce:

Date : _________________ mon tue wed thu fri sat sun

	Breakfast	Lunch	Dinner
Monday			
Tuesday			
Wednesday			
Thursaday			
Friday			
Saturday			
Sunday			

Meat :   Dairy :   Others:

Shopping
List

Produce:

Date : _________________________ mon tue wed thu fri sat sun

	Breakfast	Lunch	Dinner
Monday			
Tuesday			
Wednesday			
Thursaday			
Friday			
Saturday			
Sunday			

Meat :   Dairy :   Others:

Shopping
List

Produce:

Date : _________________ mon tue wed thu fri sat sun

	Breakfast	Lunch	Dinner
Monday			
Tuesday			
Wednesday			
Thursaday			
Friday			
Saturday			
Sunday			

Shopping List

Meat :   Dairy :   Others:

Produce:

Date : ________________ mon tue wed thu fri sat sun

	Breakfast	Lunch	Dinner
Monday			
Tuesday			
Wednesday			
Thursaday			
Friday			
Saturday			
Sunday			

Meat :   Dairy :   Others:

Shopping
List

Produce:

Date : _________________ mon tue wed thu fri sat sun

	Breakfast	Lunch	Dinner
Monday			
Tuesday			
Wednesday			
Thursaday			
Friday			
Saturday			
Sunday			

Shopping List

Meat :   Dairy :   Others:

Produce:

Date : _________________ mon tue wed thu fri sat sun

	Breakfast	Lunch	Dinner
Monday			
Tuesday			
Wednesday			
Thursaday			
Friday			
Saturday			
Sunday			

Shopping List

Meat :   Dairy :   Others:

Produce:

Date : _______________________ mon tue wed thu fri sat sun

	Breakfast	Lunch	Dinner
Monday			
Tuesday			
Wednesday			
Thursaday			
Friday			
Saturday			
Sunday			

Shopping List

Meat :   Dairy :   Others:

Produce:

Date : _________________ mon tue wed thu fri sat sun

	Breakfast	Lunch	Dinner
Monday			
Tuesday			
Wednesday			
Thursaday			
Friday			
Saturday			
Sunday			

Shopping
List

Meat :   Dairy :   Others:

Produce:

Date : _________________ mon tue wed thu fri sat sun

	Breakfast	Lunch	Dinner
Monday			
Tuesday			
Wednesday			
Thursaday			
Friday			
Saturday			
Sunday			

Shopping List

Meat :

Dairy :

Others:

Produce:

Date : _________________ mon tue wed thu fri sat sun

	Breakfast	Lunch	Dinner
Monday			
Tuesday			
Wednesday			
Thursaday			
Friday			
Saturday			
Sunday			

Shopping
List

Meat :   Dairy :   Others:

Produce:

Date : _________________ mon tue wed thu fri sat sun

	Breakfast	Lunch	Dinner
Monday			
Tuesday			
Wednesday			
Thursaday			
Friday			
Saturday			
Sunday			

Shopping
List

Meat :

Dairy :

Others:

Produce:

Date : _________________________ mon tue wed thu fri sat sun

	Breakfast	Lunch	Dinner
Monday			
Tuesday			
Wednesday			
Thursaday			
Friday			
Saturday			
Sunday			

Shopping List

Meat :   Dairy :   Others:

Produce:

Date : _________________________ mon tue wed thu fri sat sun

	Breakfast	Lunch	Dinner
Monday			
Tuesday			
Wednesday			
Thursaday			
Friday			
Saturday			
Sunday			

Shopping List

Meat :   Dairy :   Others:

Produce:

Date : _________________ mon tue wed thu fri sat sun

	Breakfast	Lunch	Dinner
Monday			
Tuesday			
Wednesday			
Thursaday			
Friday			
Saturday			
Sunday			

Shopping List

Meat :   Dairy :   Others:

Produce:

Date : _________________ mon tue wed thu fri sat sun

	Breakfast	Lunch	Dinner
Monday			
Tuesday			
Wednesday			
Thursaday			
Friday			
Saturday			
Sunday			

Meat :   Dairy :   Others:

Shopping
List

Produce:

Date : _________________ mon tue wed thu fri sat sun

	Breakfast	Lunch	Dinner
Monday			
Tuesday			
Wednesday			
Thursaday			
Friday			
Saturday			
Sunday			

Shopping List

Meat :   Dairy :   Others:

Produce:

Date : _________________________ mon tue wed thu fri sat sun

	Breakfast	Lunch	Dinner
Monday			
Tuesday			
Wednesday			
Thursaday			
Friday			
Saturday			
Sunday			

Shopping List

Meat :   Dairy :   Others:

Produce:

Date : ___________________ mon tue wed thu fri sat sun

	Breakfast	Lunch	Dinner
Monday			
Tuesday			
Wednesday			
Thursaday			
Friday			
Saturday			
Sunday			

Shopping
List

Meat :   Dairy :   Others:

Produce:

Date : _______________ mon tue wed thu fri sat sun

	Breakfast	Lunch	Dinner
Monday			
Tuesday			
Wednesday			
Thursaday			
Friday			
Saturday			
Sunday			

Shopping List

Meat :

Dairy :

Others:

Produce:

Date : _________________ mon tue wed thu fri sat sun

	Breakfast	Lunch	Dinner
Monday			
Tuesday			
Wednesday			
Thursaday			
Friday			
Saturday			
Sunday			

Shopping
List

Meat :   Dairy :   Others:

Produce:

Date : _________________ mon tue wed thu fri sat sun

	Breakfast	Lunch	Dinner
Monday			
Tuesday			
Wednesday			
Thursaday			
Friday			
Saturday			
Sunday			

Shopping
List

Meat :   Dairy :   Others:

Produce:

Date : _________________________ mon tue wed thu fri sat sun

	Breakfast	Lunch	Dinner
Monday			
Tuesday			
Wednesday			
Thursaday			
Friday			
Saturday			
Sunday			

Shopping List

Meat :   Dairy :   Others:

Produce:

Date : _________________ mon tue wed thu fri sat sun

	Breakfast	Lunch	Dinner
Monday			
Tuesday			
Wednesday			
Thursaday			
Friday			
Saturday			
Sunday			

Shopping
List

Meat :

Dairy :

Others:

Produce:

Date : ________________________ mon tue wed thu fri sat sun

	Breakfast	Lunch	Dinner
Monday			
Tuesday			
Wednesday			
Thursaday			
Friday			
Saturday			
Sunday			

Shopping
List

Meat :   Dairy :   Others:

Produce:

Date : _________________ mon tue wed thu fri sat sun

	Breakfast	Lunch	Dinner
Monday			
Tuesday			
Wednesday			
Thursaday			
Friday			
Saturday			
Sunday			

Shopping
List

Meat :   Dairy :   Others:

Produce:

Date : _________________________ mon tue wed thu fri sat sun

	Breakfast	Lunch	Dinner
Monday			
Tuesday			
Wednesday			
Thursaday			
Friday			
Saturday			
Sunday			

Shopping List

Meat :   Dairy :   Others:

Produce:

Date : _________________________ mon tue wed thu fri sat sun

	Breakfast	Lunch	Dinner
Monday			
Tuesday			
Wednesday			
Thursaday			
Friday			
Saturday			
Sunday			

Shopping
List

Meat :   Dairy :   Others:

Produce:

Date : _________________________ mon tue wed thu fri sat sun

	Breakfast	Lunch	Dinner
Monday			
Tuesday			
Wednesday			
Thursaday			
Friday			
Saturday			
Sunday			

Shopping List

Meat :   Dairy :   Others:

Produce:

Date : _________________ mon tue wed thu fri sat sun

	Breakfast	Lunch	Dinner
Monday			
Tuesday			
Wednesday			
Thursaday			
Friday			
Saturday			
Sunday			

Meat :   Dairy :   Others:

Shopping
List

Produce:

Date : _________________________ mon tue wed thu fri sat sun

	Breakfast	Lunch	Dinner
Monday			
Tuesday			
Wednesday			
Thursaday			
Friday			
Saturday			
Sunday			

Shopping
List

Meat :   Dairy :   Others:

Produce:

Date : _________________ mon tue wed thu fri sat sun

	Breakfast	Lunch	Dinner
Monday			
Tuesday			
Wednesday			
Thursaday			
Friday			
Saturday			
Sunday			

Shopping List

Meat :

Dairy :

Others:

Produce:

Date : ___________________ mon tue wed thu fri sat sun

	Breakfast	Lunch	Dinner
Monday			
Tuesday			
Wednesday			
Thursaday			
Friday			
Saturday			
Sunday			

Shopping
List

Meat :   Dairy :   Others:

Produce:

Date : _________________ mon tue wed thu fri sat sun

	Breakfast	Lunch	Dinner
Monday			
Tuesday			
Wednesday			
Thursaday			
Friday			
Saturday			
Sunday			

Shopping List

Meat :

Dairy :

Others:

Produce:

Date : _________________ mon tue wed thu fri sat sun

	Breakfast	Lunch	Dinner
Monday			
Tuesday			
Wednesday			
Thursaday			
Friday			
Saturday			
Sunday			

Meat :   Dairy :   Others:

Shopping
List

Produce:

Date : _________________ mon tue wed thu fri sat sun

	Breakfast	Lunch	Dinner
Monday			
Tuesday			
Wednesday			
Thursaday			
Friday			
Saturday			
Sunday			

Shopping
List

Meat :   Dairy :   Others:

Produce:

Date : _________________________ mon tue wed thu fri sat sun

	Breakfast	Lunch	Dinner
Monday			
Tuesday			
Wednesday			
Thursaday			
Friday			
Saturday			
Sunday			

Shopping List

Meat :   Dairy :   Others:

Produce:

Date : _________________ mon tue wed thu fri sat sun

	Breakfast	Lunch	Dinner
Monday			
Tuesday			
Wednesday			
Thursaday			
Friday			
Saturday			
Sunday			

Shopping
List

Meat :   Dairy :   Others:

Produce:

Date : _________________________ mon tue wed thu fri sat sun

	Breakfast	Lunch	Dinner
Monday			
Tuesday			
Wednesday			
Thursaday			
Friday			
Saturday			
Sunday			

Shopping List

Meat :   Dairy :   Others:

Produce:

Date : _________________ mon tue wed thu fri sat sun

	Breakfast	Lunch	Dinner
Monday			
Tuesday			
Wednesday			
Thursaday			
Friday			
Saturday			
Sunday			

Shopping List

Meat :

Dairy :

Others:

Produce:

Date : _________________________ mon tue wed thu fri sat sun

	Breakfast	Lunch	Dinner
Monday			
Tuesday			
Wednesday			
Thursaday			
Friday			
Saturday			
Sunday			

Meat :   Dairy :   Others:

Shopping
List

Produce:

Date : ________________________ mon tue wed thu fri sat sun

	Breakfast	Lunch	Dinner
Monday			
Tuesday			
Wednesday			
Thursaday			
Friday			
Saturday			
Sunday			

Shopping List

Meat :   Dairy :   Others:

Produce:

Date : _________________ mon tue wed thu fri sat sun

	Breakfast	Lunch	Dinner
Monday			
Tuesday			
Wednesday			
Thursaday			
Friday			
Saturday			
Sunday			

Shopping List

Meat :

Dairy :

Others:

Produce:

Date : _________________________ mon tue wed thu fri sat sun

	Breakfast	Lunch	Dinner
Monday			
Tuesday			
Wednesday			
Thursaday			
Friday			
Saturday			
Sunday			

Shopping List

Meat :   Dairy :   Others:

Produce:

Date : _________________ mon tue wed thu fri sat sun

	Breakfast	Lunch	Dinner
Monday			
Tuesday			
Wednesday			
Thursaday			
Friday			
Saturday			
Sunday			

Shopping
List

Meat :   Dairy :   Others:

Produce:

Date : _________________ mon tue wed thu fri sat sun

	Breakfast	Lunch	Dinner
Monday			
Tuesday			
Wednesday			
Thursaday			
Friday			
Saturday			
Sunday			

Shopping List

Meat :   Dairy :   Others:

Produce:

Date : ________________ mon tue wed thu fri sat sun

	Breakfast	Lunch	Dinner
Monday			
Tuesday			
Wednesday			
Thursaday			
Friday			
Saturday			
Sunday			

Shopping
List

Meat :   Dairy :   Others:

Produce:

Date : _________________ mon tue wed thu fri sat sun

	Breakfast	Lunch	Dinner
Monday			
Tuesday			
Wednesday			
Thursaday			
Friday			
Saturday			
Sunday			

Meat :   Dairy :   Others:

Shopping List

Produce:

Date : _________________ mon tue wed thu fri sat sun

	Breakfast	Lunch	Dinner
Monday			
Tuesday			
Wednesday			
Thursaday			
Friday			
Saturday			
Sunday			

Shopping
List

Meat :   Dairy :   Others:

Produce:

Date : _________________ mon tue wed thu fri sat sun

	Breakfast	Lunch	Dinner
Monday			
Tuesday			
Wednesday			
Thursaday			
Friday			
Saturday			
Sunday			

Shopping
List

Meat :   Dairy :   Others:

Produce:

Date : _________________ mon tue wed thu fri sat sun

	Breakfast	Lunch	Dinner
Monday			
Tuesday			
Wednesday			
Thursaday			
Friday			
Saturday			
Sunday			

Shopping List

Meat :   Dairy :   Others:

Produce:

Date : _________________ mon tue wed thu fri sat sun

	Breakfast	Lunch	Dinner
Monday			
Tuesday			
Wednesday			
Thursaday			
Friday			
Saturday			
Sunday			

Shopping
List

Meat :   Dairy :   Others:

Produce:

Date : _________________________ mon tue wed thu fri sat sun

	Breakfast	Lunch	Dinner
Monday			
Tuesday			
Wednesday			
Thursaday			
Friday			
Saturday			
Sunday			

Shopping List

Meat :   Dairy :   Others:

Produce:

Date : _________________ mon tue wed thu fri sat sun

	Breakfast	Lunch	Dinner
Monday			
Tuesday			
Wednesday			
Thursaday			
Friday			
Saturday			
Sunday			

Shopping List

Meat :   Dairy :   Others:

Produce:

Date : _________________________ mon tue wed thu fri sat sun

	Breakfast	Lunch	Dinner
Monday			
Tuesday			
Wednesday			
Thursaday			
Friday			
Saturday			
Sunday			

Shopping List

Meat :   Dairy :   Others:

Produce:

Date : _________________ mon tue wed thu fri sat sun

	Breakfast	Lunch	Dinner
Monday			
Tuesday			
Wednesday			
Thursaday			
Friday			
Saturday			
Sunday			

Shopping List

Meat :

Dairy :

Others:

Produce:

Date : ________________________ mon tue wed thu fri sat sun

	Breakfast	Lunch	Dinner
Monday			
Tuesday			
Wednesday			
Thursaday			
Friday			
Saturday			
Sunday			

Shopping List

Meat :   Dairy :   Others:

Produce:

Date : _________________ mon tue wed thu fri sat sun

	Breakfast	Lunch	Dinner
Monday			
Tuesday			
Wednesday			
Thursaday			
Friday			
Saturday			
Sunday			

Shopping List

Meat :   Dairy :   Others:

Produce:

Date : _________________ mon tue wed thu fri sat sun

	Breakfast	Lunch	Dinner
Monday			
Tuesday			
Wednesday			
Thursaday			
Friday			
Saturday			
Sunday			

Shopping List

Meat :

Dairy :

Others:

Produce:

Date : _________________ mon tue wed thu fri sat sun

	Breakfast	Lunch	Dinner
Monday			
Tuesday			
Wednesday			
Thursaday			
Friday			
Saturday			
Sunday			

Shopping
List

Meat :   Dairy :   Others:

Produce:

Date : _________________ *mon tue wed thu fri sat sun*

	Breakfast	Lunch	Dinner
Monday			
Tuesday			
Wednesday			
Thursaday			
Friday			
Saturday			
Sunday			

Shopping List

Meat :   Dairy :   Others:

Produce:

Date : ________________________ mon tue wed thu fri sat sun

	Breakfast	Lunch	Dinner
Monday			
Tuesday			
Wednesday			
Thursaday			
Friday			
Saturday			
Sunday			

Shopping List

Meat :   Dairy :   Others:

Produce:

Date : _____________________ mon tue wed thu fri sat sun

	Breakfast	Lunch	Dinner
Monday			
Tuesday			
Wednesday			
Thursaday			
Friday			
Saturday			
Sunday			

Shopping List

Meat :   Dairy :   Others:

Produce:

Date : _________________ mon tue wed thu fri sat sun

	Breakfast	Lunch	Dinner
Monday			
Tuesday			
Wednesday			
Thursaday			
Friday			
Saturday			
Sunday			

Meat :   Dairy :   Others:

Shopping List

Produce:

Date : _________________ mon tue wed thu fri sat sun

	Breakfast	Lunch	Dinner
Monday			
Tuesday			
Wednesday			
Thursaday			
Friday			
Saturday			
Sunday			

Shopping
List

Meat :   Dairy :   Others:

Produce:

Date : _________________ mon tue wed thu fri sat sun

	Breakfast	Lunch	Dinner
Monday			
Tuesday			
Wednesday			
Thursaday			
Friday			
Saturday			
Sunday			

Shopping List

Meat :   Dairy :   Others:

Produce:

Date : ___________________ mon tue wed thu fri sat sun

	Breakfast	Lunch	Dinner
Monday			
Tuesday			
Wednesday			
Thursaday			
Friday			
Saturday			
Sunday			

Shopping
List

Meat :   Dairy :   Others:

Produce:

Date : _________________ mon tue wed thu fri sat sun

	Breakfast	Lunch	Dinner
Monday			
Tuesday			
Wednesday			
Thursaday			
Friday			
Saturday			
Sunday			

Shopping List

Meat :

Dairy :

Others:

Produce:

Date : _________________________ mon tue wed thu fri sat sun

	Breakfast	Lunch	Dinner
Monday			
Tuesday			
Wednesday			
Thursaday			
Friday			
Saturday			
Sunday			

Shopping
List

Meat :

Dairy :

Others:

Produce:

Date : ___________________ mon tue wed thu fri sat sun

	Breakfast	Lunch	Dinner
Monday			
Tuesday			
Wednesday			
Thursaday			
Friday			
Saturday			
Sunday			

Shopping
List

Meat :   Dairy :   Others:

Produce:

Date : _________________ mon tue wed thu fri sat sun

	Breakfast	Lunch	Dinner
Monday			
Tuesday			
Wednesday			
Thursaday			
Friday			
Saturday			
Sunday			

Shopping
List

Meat :   Dairy :   Others:

Produce:

Date : _________________ mon tue wed thu fri sat sun

	Breakfast	Lunch	Dinner
Monday			
Tuesday			
Wednesday			
Thursaday			
Friday			
Saturday			
Sunday			

Shopping
List

Meat :   Dairy :   Others:

Produce:

Date : _________________ mon tue wed thu fri sat sun

	Breakfast	Lunch	Dinner
Monday			
Tuesday			
Wednesday			
Thursaday			
Friday			
Saturday			
Sunday			

Shopping List

Meat :

Dairy :

Others:

Produce:

Date : _________________ mon tue wed thu fri sat sun

	Breakfast	Lunch	Dinner
Monday			
Tuesday			
Wednesday			
Thursaday			
Friday			
Saturday			
Sunday			

Shopping List

Meat :   Dairy :   Others:

Produce:

Date : _________________ mon tue wed thu fri sat sun

	Breakfast	Lunch	Dinner
Monday			
Tuesday			
Wednesday			
Thursaday			
Friday			
Saturday			
Sunday			

Shopping List

Meat :

Dairy :

Others:

Produce:

Date : _________________ mon tue wed thu fri sat sun

	Breakfast	Lunch	Dinner
Monday			
Tuesday			
Wednesday			
Thursaday			
Friday			
Saturday			
Sunday			

Shopping
List

Meat :   Dairy :   Others:

Produce:

Date : _________________ mon tue wed thu fri sat sun

	Breakfast	Lunch	Dinner
Monday			
Tuesday			
Wednesday			
Thursaday			
Friday			
Saturday			
Sunday			

Shopping
List

Meat :   Dairy :   Others:

Produce:

Date : _________________ mon tue wed thu fri sat sun

	Breakfast	Lunch	Dinner
Monday			
Tuesday			
Wednesday			
Thursaday			
Friday			
Saturday			
Sunday			

Shopping List

Meat :   Dairy :   Others:

Produce:

Date : _________________________ mon tue wed thu fri sat sun

	Breakfast	Lunch	Dinner
Monday			
Tuesday			
Wednesday			
Thursaday			
Friday			
Saturday			
Sunday			

Shopping List

Meat :   Dairy :   Others:

Produce:

Date : _________________________ mon tue wed thu fri sat sun

	Breakfast	Lunch	Dinner
Monday			
Tuesday			
Wednesday			
Thursaday			
Friday			
Saturday			
Sunday			

Shopping
List

Meat :   Dairy :   Others:

Produce:

Date : _________________ mon tue wed thu fri sat sun

	Breakfast	Lunch	Dinner
Monday			
Tuesday			
Wednesday			
Thursaday			
Friday			
Saturday			
Sunday			

Shopping List

Meat :   Dairy :   Others:

Produce:

Date : _________________ *mon tue wed thu fri sat sun*

	Breakfast	Lunch	Dinner
Monday			
Tuesday			
Wednesday			
Thursaday			
Friday			
Saturday			
Sunday			

Shopping List

Meat :   Dairy :   Others:

Produce:

Date : _________________ mon tue wed thu fri sat sun

	Breakfast	Lunch	Dinner
Monday			
Tuesday			
Wednesday			
Thursaday			
Friday			
Saturday			
Sunday			

Shopping List

Meat :   Dairy :   Others:

Produce:

Date : _________________ *mon tue wed thu fri sat sun*

	Breakfast	Lunch	Dinner
Monday			
Tuesday			
Wednesday			
Thursaday			
Friday			
Saturday			
Sunday			

Shopping List

Meat :   Dairy :   Others:

Produce:

Date : ___________________ mon tue wed thu fri sat sun

	Breakfast	Lunch	Dinner
Monday			
Tuesday			
Wednesday			
Thursaday			
Friday			
Saturday			
Sunday			

Shopping List

Meat :   Dairy :   Others:

Produce:

Date : _________________________ *mon tue wed thu fri sat sun*

	Breakfast	Lunch	Dinner
Monday			
Tuesday			
Wednesday			
Thursaday			
Friday			
Saturday			
Sunday			

Shopping List

Meat :

Dairy :

Others:

Produce:

Date : _________________ mon tue wed thu fri sat sun

	Breakfast	Lunch	Dinner
Monday			
Tuesday			
Wednesday			
Thursaday			
Friday			
Saturday			
Sunday			

Shopping
List

Meat :   Dairy :   Others:

Produce:

Date : _________________ mon tue wed thu fri sat sun

	Breakfast	Lunch	Dinner
Monday			
Tuesday			
Wednesday			
Thursaday			
Friday			
Saturday			
Sunday			

Shopping List

Meat :   Dairy :   Others:

Produce:

Date : ________________ mon tue wed thu fri sat sun

	Breakfast	Lunch	Dinner
Monday			
Tuesday			
Wednesday			
Thursaday			
Friday			
Saturday			
Sunday			

Shopping
List

Meat :   Dairy :   Others:

Produce:

www.ingramcontent.com/pod-product-compliance
Lightning Source LLC
Chambersburg PA
CBHW081311250726
48662CB00008B/2504